Contents

About this book

Most of the work in this book is for you to do on your own.

Sometimes you will work with a friend.

You will need instructions from your teacher to do some of the work.

Sometimes you need things to help you. The pictures at the bottom of each page show you what you need.

pencil

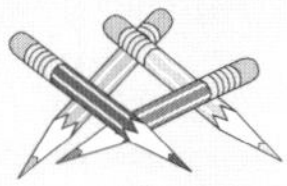

coloured pencils

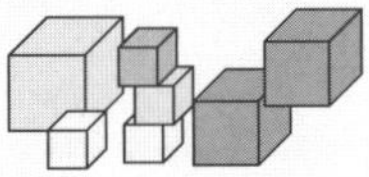

cubes

dominoes

money

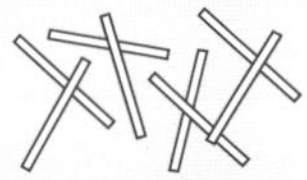

matchsticks

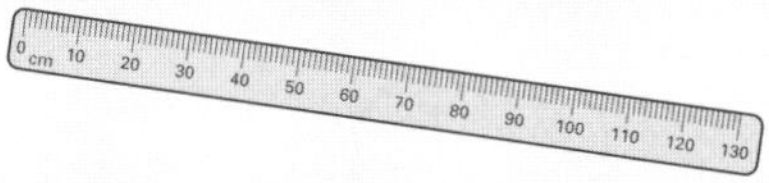

ruler

number cards

At the bottom of some pages, there is extra work your teacher might ask you to do. It has a key next to it, like this: 

Work carefully! Read each question all the way through before trying to work out the answer.

Do not write in this book.

Ordering numbers

Order the sets of numbers, largest first.

1\. 119, 345, 429, 210, 492, 201, 249, 109, 942, 354, 881, 191, 818

2\. 1539, 401, 224, 358, 967, 410, 1976, 540, 616, 1060, 661

Now write the largest number in each set in words

Order the sets of numbers, smallest first.

3\. 618, 261, 109, 168, 126, 201, 681, 191, 99, 162, 861, 422

4\. 670, 896, 954, 4371, 251, 763, 6070, 127, 281, 505, 671, 617, 406

Now write the smallest number in each set in words

Write the largest number on the page in words.

Snails going home (1)

The snails want to go to the woods where they live.

They have to go through the garden to get there. There are flowers growing in the gardens. The number in each garden shows how many flowers there are.

The snails love eating flowers.

Investigate

Which route will give the snails the most flowers?

They can travel vertically, horizontally or diagonally. They cannot jump a garden. They must not move backwards.

Record your answers as additions.

Example 10 + 16 + 12 + 53 + 35 = 126

Which route will give the fewest flowers?

How many different routes can you find?

Snails going home (2)

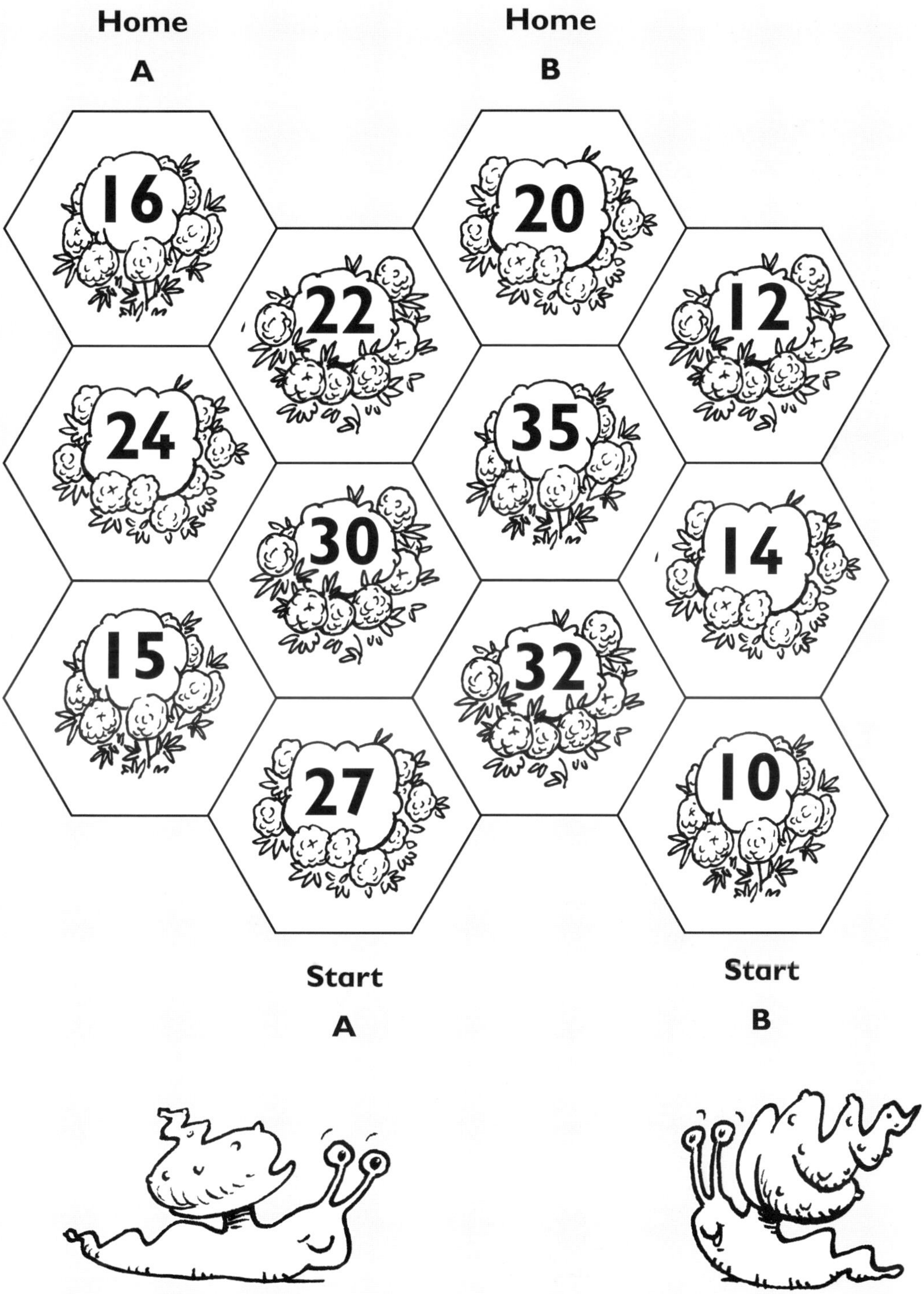

Can you find the route with the total closest to 100?
To 150? To 200?

Burger Bar (1)

Betty's * Burgers

Plain burger £1·20	Cola 45p
Cheeseburger £1·50	Ice cream 40p
Triple burger £1·75	Salad 50p
Fish burger £1·50	Chips 50p
Vege burger £1·20	Choc bar 25p

1. What could you buy for £2·50?
   What change would you get?
   Write three combinations.
   Example fish burger £1·50 + salad 50p + drink 45p = £2.45
   5p change

2. What could you buy for £3·00?
   What change would you get?
   Write three combinations.

3. What could you buy for £1·75?
   What change would you get?
   Write three combinations

4. How many cheeseburgers could you buy for £5·00?
   Would you have enough change to buy something else as well?

How much would it cost to buy two of each item?

Burger Bar (2)

The till in the Burger Bar has broken down and there are lots of mistakes in the bills. The staff need your help!

Copy the bills, check them and put them right

1.

1 fish burger	£1·50
1 chips	50p
1 cola	45p
Total	£3·00

2.

1 salad	50p
1 cola	45p
1 choc bar	25p
1 chips	50p
Total	£1·90

3.

2 plain burgers	£2·50
2 chips	£1·00
2 colas	£1·00
Total	£4·50

4.

1 salad	50p
1 triple burger	£1·75
1 chips	50p
1 choc bar	25p
Total	£3·50

5.

3 cheeseburgers	£5·00
2 chips	£1·00
2 colas	90p
2 ice creams	£1·00
Total	£7·00

6.

1 fish burger	£1·50
1 chips	50p
1 salad	50p
1 ice cream	40p
1 choc bar	25p
1 cola	45p
Total	£3·00

Make up your own bills with mistakes for a friend.

Pinboard shapes

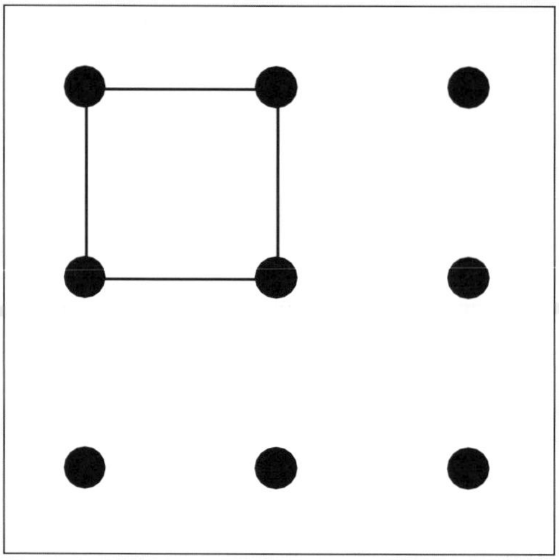

This is one of the squares you can make on a 3×3 pinboard.

How many more squares can you make?

Can you find 6?

You have a 4×4 pinboard.

How many squares can you make?

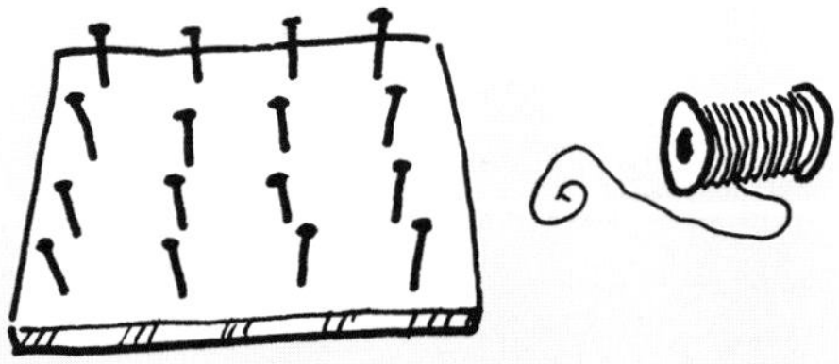

You have a 5×5 pinboard.

How many squares can you make?

It may help to use dotted paper, different coloured pens or pencils to record your answers.

How many different triangles can you make on a 3×3 pinboard?

Number buttons

Use the numbers and signs on the buttons to make each screen number. You can use each button as many times as you like. Write your calculations in your book.

Example

$10 - 2 = 8$

$8 \times 5 = 40$

$40 + 3 = 43$

1.

2.

3.

4.

5.

6.

7.

8.

9.

Now can you find a different way of making each number?

Number schemes

Copy these schemes into your workbook.

Look carefully at the arrows → ↓

Fill in the missing numbers.

1.

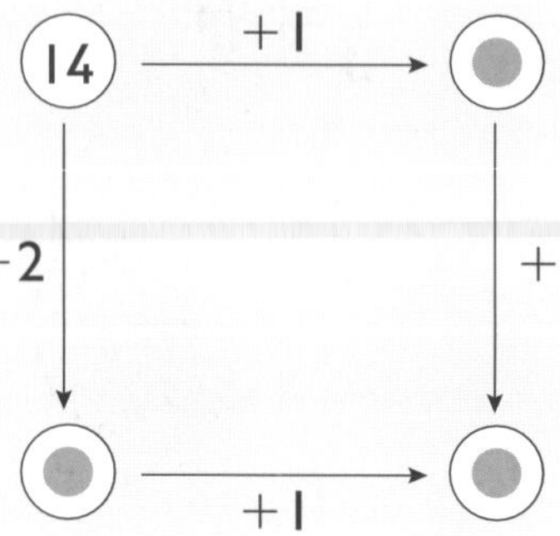

2.

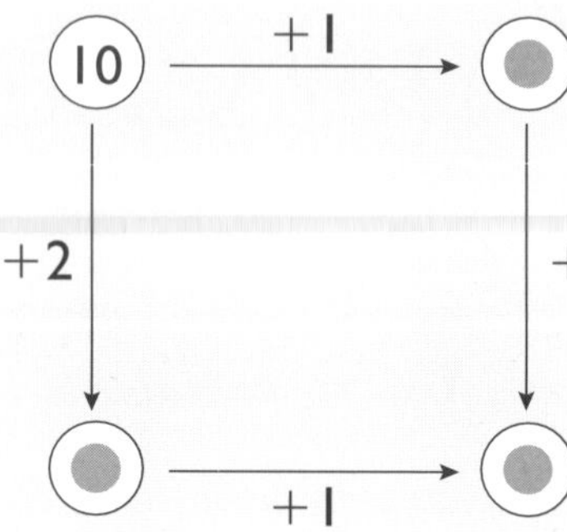

3.

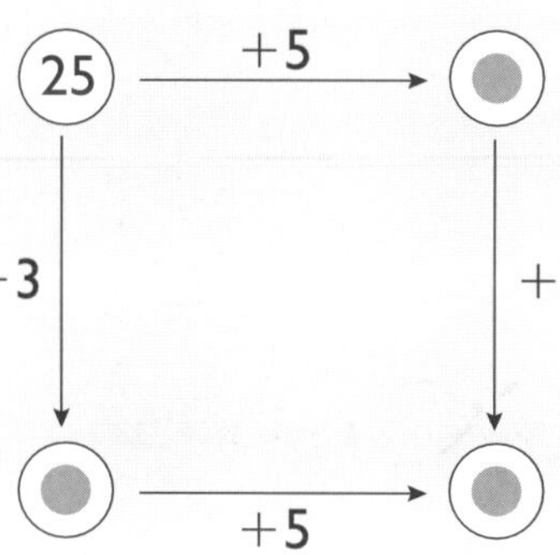

4.

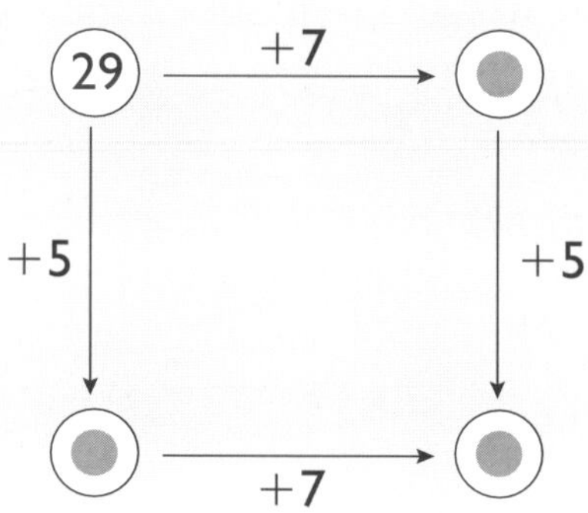

5.

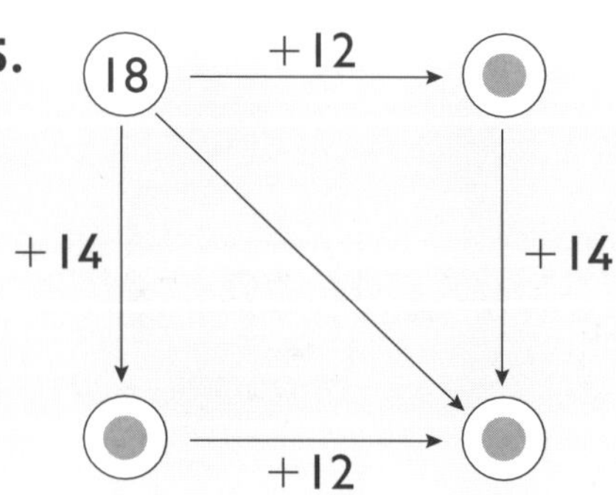

6.

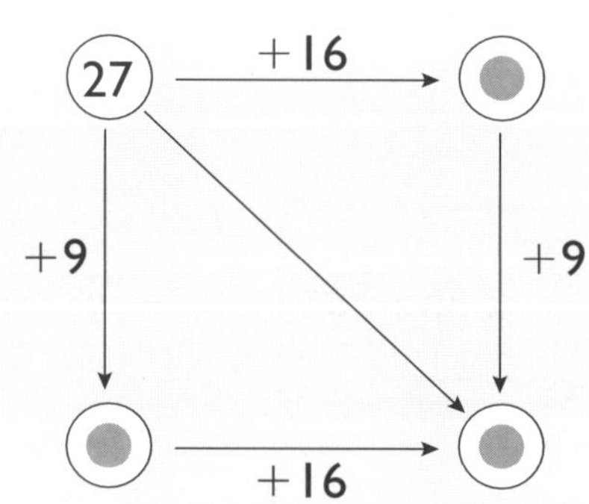

What do the diagonals mean? What happens when you follow them?

Can you make your own square?

Now make a square which uses subtraction.

Find forty

Look at this grid.

12	7	17	8	15	3	6
9	12	16	5	20	2	28
8	14	12	7	16	9	30
6	12	12	22	3	15	9
19	15	22	0	15	3	13
5	5	17	15	9	6	18

Hidden in it are seven 2 × 2 sets of numbers that add up to 40.

Example 12 + 7 + 9 + 12 = 40.

Can you find the other six sets?

Write down the additions.

What is the smallest 2 × 2 total you can make? What is the largest?

Bookshop

£3·00

£1·50

£4·00

£2·70

£2·00

£1·20

£1·30

£5·00

What combinations of books could you buy for £10·00?

You do not need to spend exactly £10·00, but you must not spend more than that.

Write down your answers and the additions.

What change would you have in each case?

What combinations could you buy for £20·00?

Circle investigation

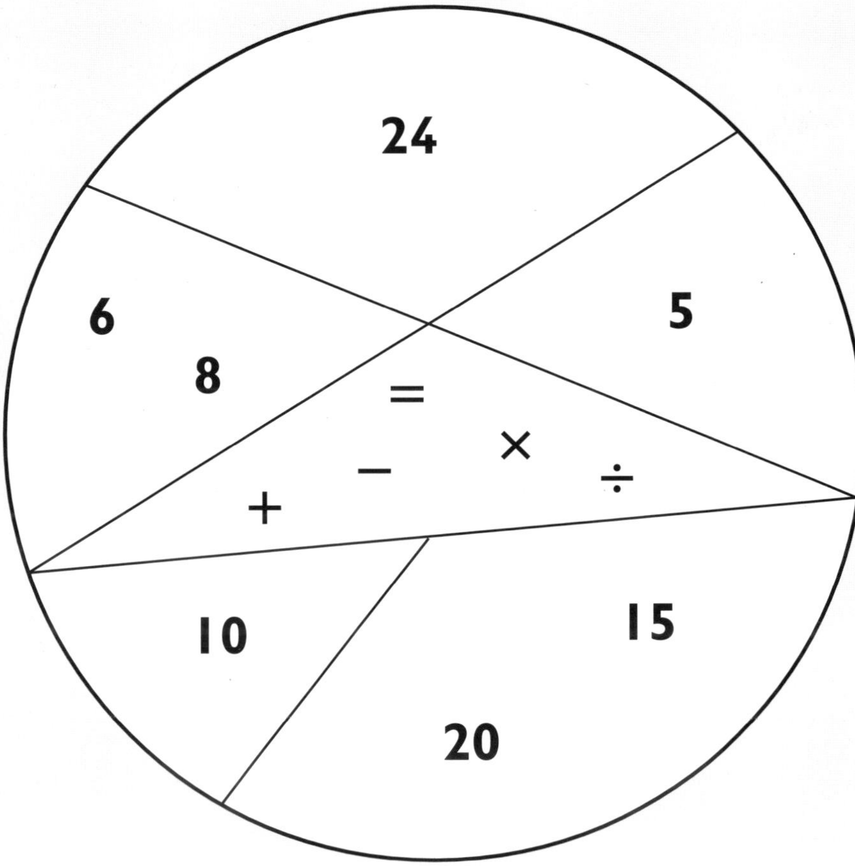

Use numbers from two different sections of the circle and the symbols +, −, ×, ÷ and = to make a sum.

Example 20 ÷ 10 = 2

What answers can you make?

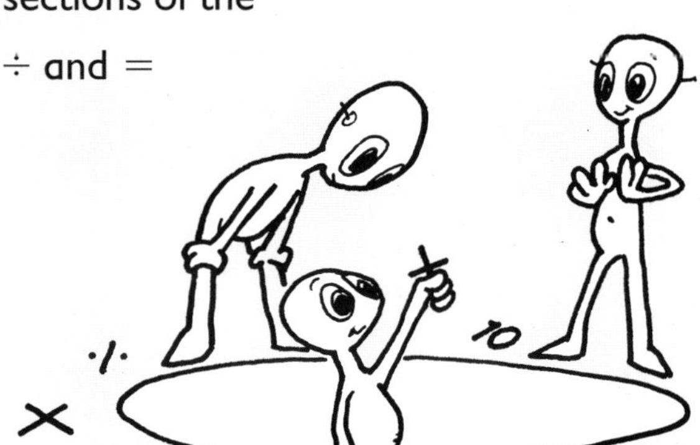

Create your own circle like the one here.
What answers can you make?

Fractions

How much of each shape is shaded?

Write the fraction.

Example 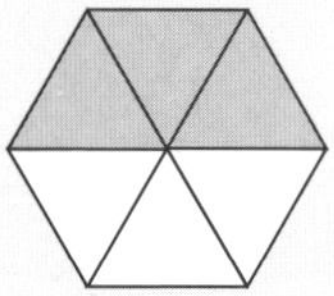 $\frac{3}{6}$ or $\frac{1}{2}$

1. 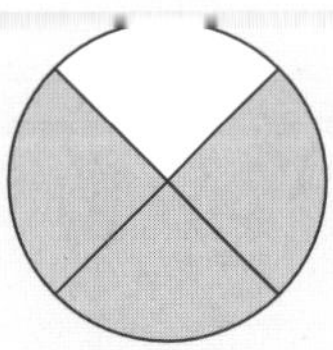

2. 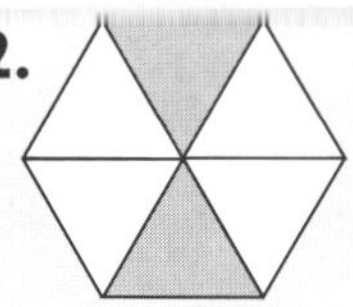

3. 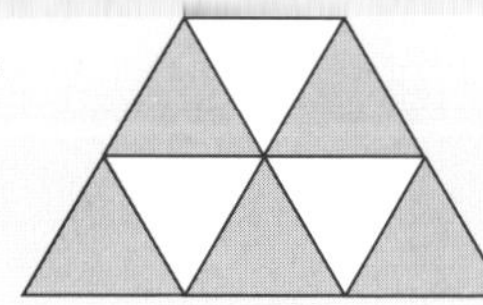

4. 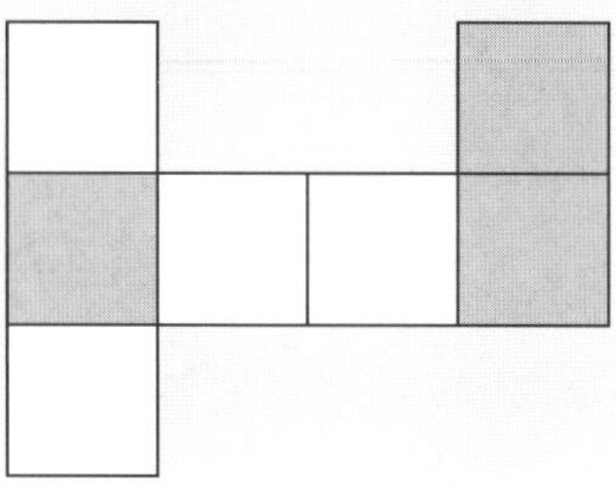

5. 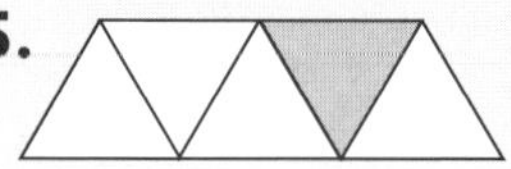

6. 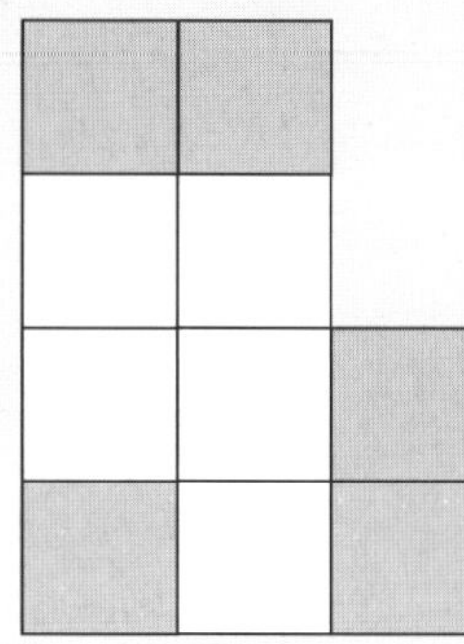

7. 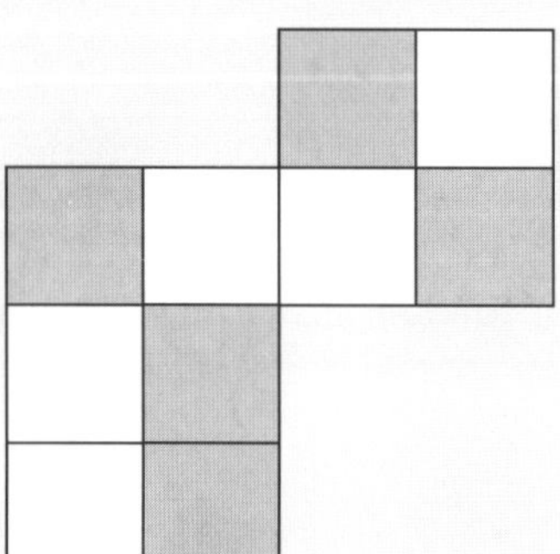

8. 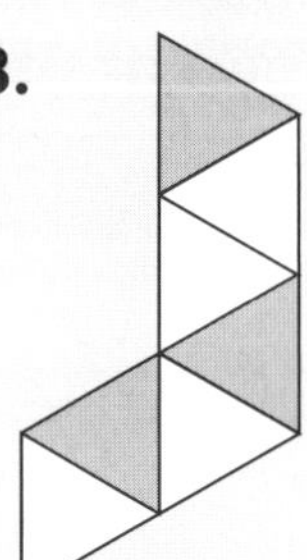

9. 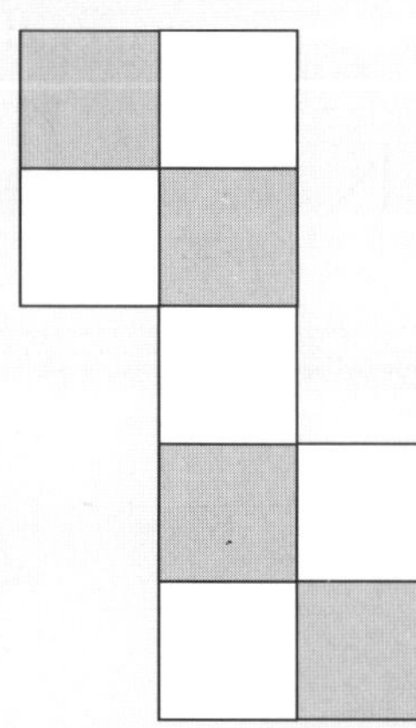

More fractions

Write $\frac{1}{4}$ of each number.

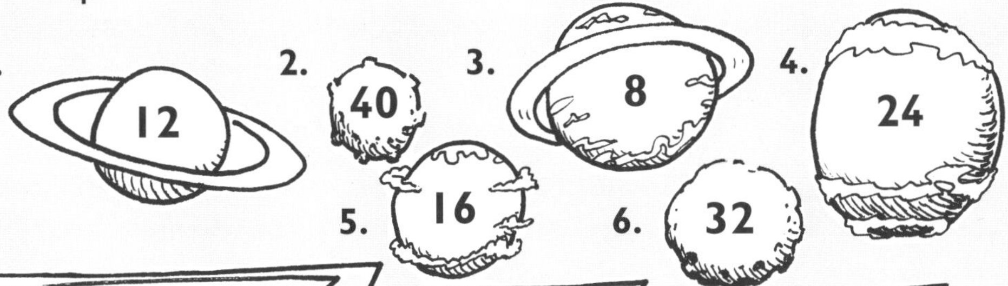

Write $\frac{1}{3}$ of each number.

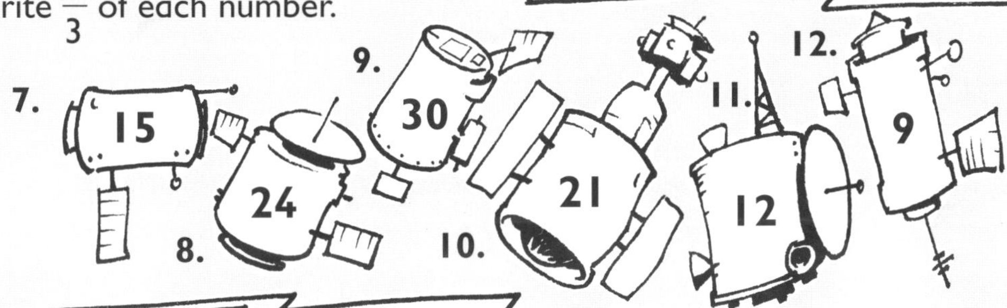

Write $\frac{1}{5}$ of each number.

Write $\frac{1}{10}$, $\frac{2}{10}$ and $\frac{3}{10}$ of each number.

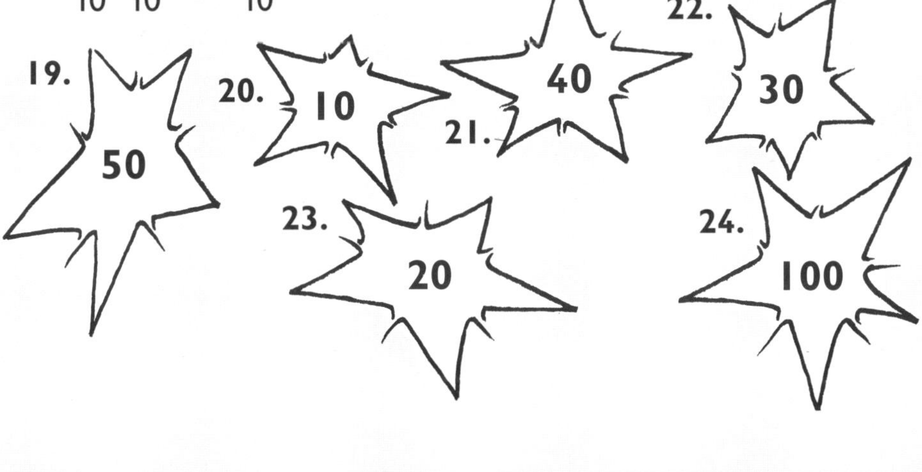

Carroll diagrams

1. Copy this Carroll diagram. You will need to draw it much bigger than it is here.

	odd	not odd
less than 20		
20 or more		

Sort this set of numbers into the correct parts of the diagram:

2 17 28 37 3 29 41 16 68 83 5 19 79 1 110

2. Copy this Carroll diagram. You will need to draw it much bigger than it is here.

	even	not even
less than 30		
30 or more		

Sort this set of numbers into the correct parts of the diagram.

100 13 63 28 12 88 99 54 10 19 17 51 20

37 16 98 115 4

3. Make a Carroll diagram with your own labels.

Put some numbers in each box.

Matching numbers

1. Copy these numbers and write them in words.

832 273 697 104 1703 956 402 518

888 1414 199 1864 1929

2. Copy these numbers and write them in figures.

nine hundred and sixty-two

one thousand three hundred and forty-one

five hundred and sixty-five

ninety-nine

one thousand nine hundred and nineteen

eight hundred and seventy-five

four hundred and thirty-two

one thousand and eleven

two hundred and forty-six

one hundred and fifty-two

3. Now put each set in order, largest first.

Can you put all the numbers on the page in order, smallest first?

Alien excursion

Zig, Zag and Zog are going to the seaside. To power their ships on earth they need jellybeans. Each alien has to stop and buy more along the way. How much do they each spend? Who chooses the cheapest route? Which route is the most expensive?

How much do they spend altogether?

Funfair

Coconut shy 30p

Helter skelter 50p

Dodgems 70p

Roller coaster 75p

Roundabout 80p

Big wheel 65p

Lucky dip 20p

How could you spend each amount of money?

Write out the additions and find how much money you would have left.

Example £2·00

With £2·00 I could buy a ride on the roller coaster and the roundabout.

75p + 80p = £1·55

£2·00 − £1·55 = 45p

45p left

1. £1·50 **2.** £1·00 **3.** 75p **4.** £1·75

5. 95p **6.** £2·25 **7.** £5·00 **8.** £3·00

How much would two turns on each cost?

Length

Estimate and then use a ruler to measure each distance to the nearest half centimetre.

Measure carefully.

1. a to b **2.** c to d **3.** g to h

4. a to c **5.** e to f **6.** e to i

7. c to e **8.** e to q **9.** f to q

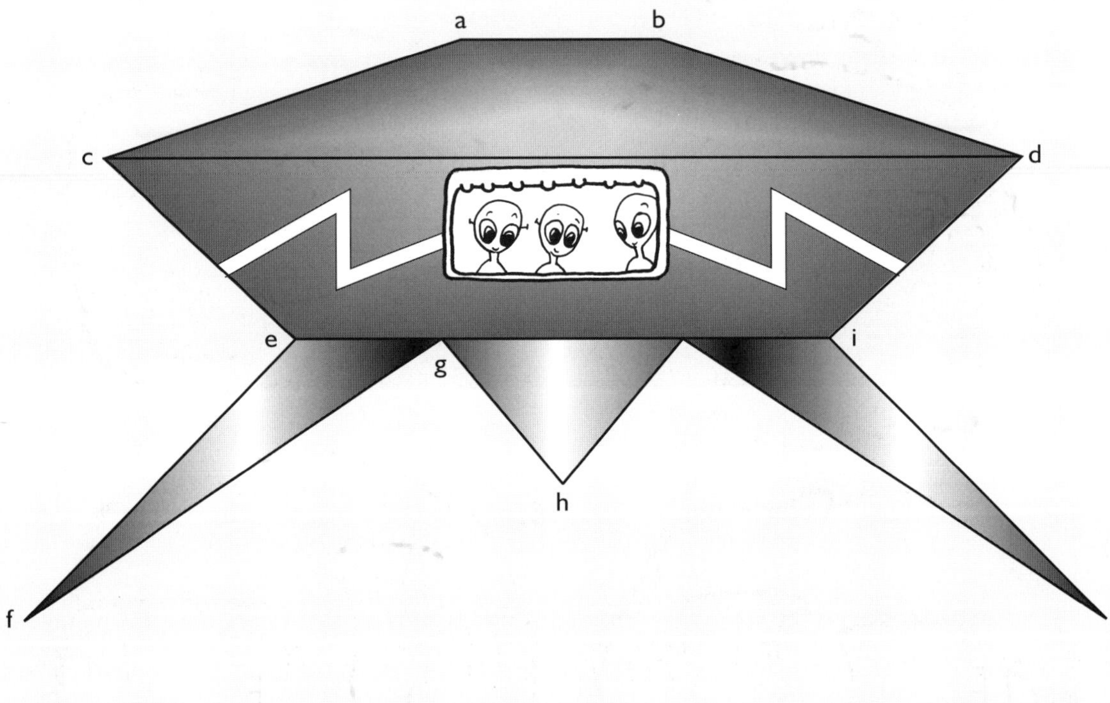

Now estimate and measure the walls and roof of the house

Capacity

How much altogether? Each jug holds 1 litre.

1.

2.

3.

4.

5.

6.

Target game

Play this game with a partner. Each pair needs a complete set of dominoes.

Place the dominoes face down on a table.
Decide on a target number between **30** and **50**.

Each player takes 5 dominoes. You must try to make the target number, using the numbers on the dominoes and the symbols $+$, $-$, $\times$ and $\div$.
You may use each number more than once.

Example

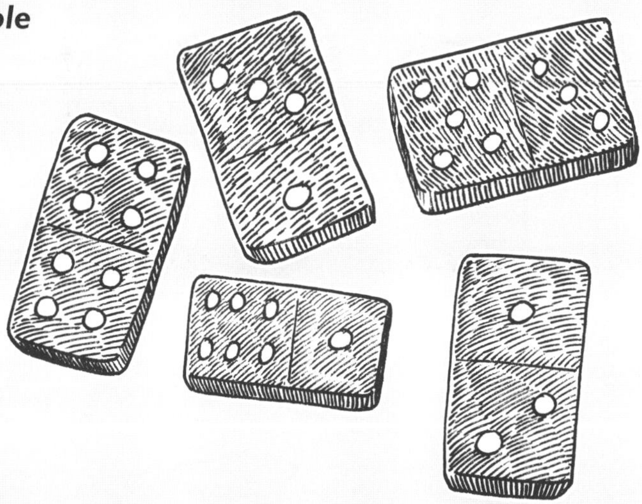

Target = 40

$(4 \times 4) + (6 \times 1) + (5 \times 3) + (2 + 1) = 40$

$16 + 6 + 15 + 3 = 40$

The first person to make the target number scores 1 point.

Change dominoes and play again.
The first to score 5 points is the winner.

Matchsticks

Work in pairs.

Each pair needs **24** sticks.

Use the 24 sticks to make a square.

Now can you use all your 24 sticks to make 5 squares?

6 squares?

3 squares?

Can you make a different number of squares using 24 sticks?

Can you find a way of making 4 squares
(2 large and 2 small) using **15** sticks?
It is possible!

Make that

Play this game with a partner. Each pair needs a set of money cards and some coins (2 × 50p, 4 × 20p, 4 × 10p, 5 × 5p).

Place the cards face down. The first player picks up a card, makes the amount shown with the coins and writes down the answer. The second player has to make the same amount in a different way. Keep taking turns to make that amount until one of you cannot think of another way. The last player to make the amount keeps the card.

Example

Card amount = £1

1st player £1 = 50p + 50p

2nd player £1 = 50p + 20p + 20p + 10p

Repeat until all the cards are used.

The player with the most cards wins.

Pick two money cards and see how many ways you can make the total amount.

Buying stamps

You have £2·00 to buy some stamps.

You can buy stamps for 13p, 10p, 20p and 22p.

Investigate what different sets of stamps you could buy and how much money you would have left.

Write out the sets and your calculations in your workbook like this.

10p + 10p + 10p = 30p

£2·00 − 30p = £1·70

£1·70 left

What is the largest number of stamps you could buy for £2·00?

Choose a different starting amount and repeat.

How much would it cost to buy three of each kind of stamp?

How much would it cost to buy five of each kind of stamp?

How much would it cost to buy ten of each kind of stamp?

Stationery shop

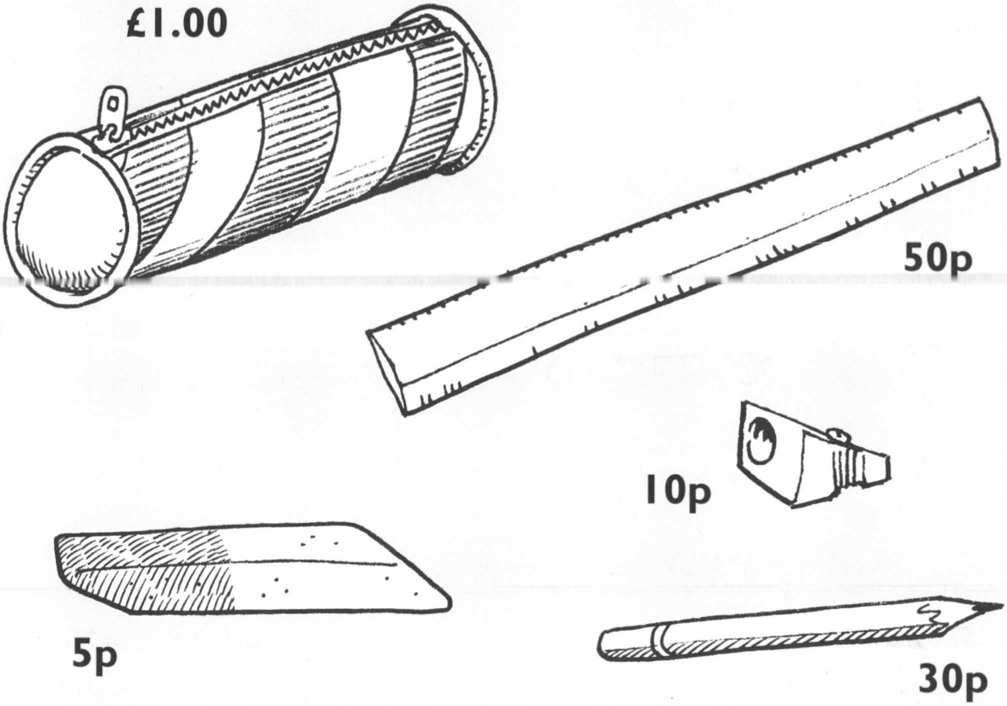

Work out how much each person has left after they have bought their stationery.

1. Randeep has £1·54. He buys two pencils.
2. Louise has £2·00. She buys a pencil case and two pencils.
3. Jeremy has £5·00. He buys two pencil cases, two rulers, two pencil sharpeners and a rubber.
4. Hilary has £3·75. She buys a pencil case and a rubber.
5. Yasser has £2·60. He buys two rulers, a pencil and a rubber.
6. Salma has £4·00. She buys five pencils, a ruler, two pencil sharpeners and two rubbers.

Imagine you have £3.00 to spend. What could you buy? How much would you have left?

More fractions

Write out these lists of equivalent fractions in full.

1. $\frac{1}{2} = \frac{2}{\ast} = \frac{3}{\ast} = \frac{\ast}{10} = \frac{\ast}{8}$

2. $\frac{1}{4} = \frac{2}{\ast} = \frac{3}{\ast} = \frac{\ast}{20}$

3. Put these fractions in order, smallest first.

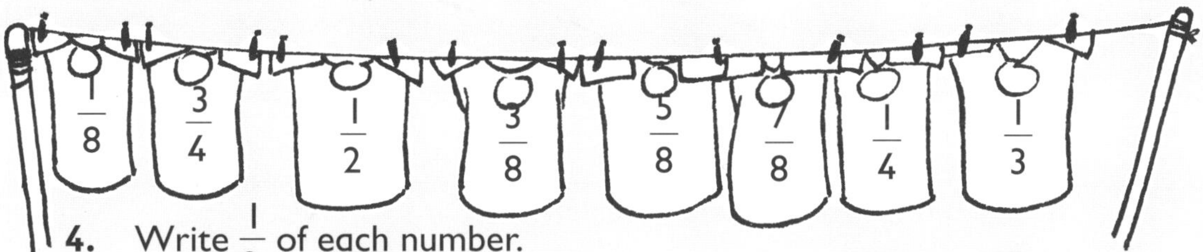

4. Write $\frac{1}{2}$ of each number.

5. Write $\frac{1}{4}$ of each number.

6. Write $\frac{3}{4}$ of each number.

7. Write $\frac{1}{2}$ and $\frac{1}{4}$ of each amount.

Now write $\frac{3}{4}$ of each amount.

Recipes

1. Double each number

6 12 9 5 7 11 8

2. Halve each number

16 4 12 8 6 10 2

3. Write each recipe out again so it makes double the amount, and then again so it makes half the amount.

Why might you need to do this?

Plain cake

100 g sugar

100 g margarine

2 eggs

150 g flour

1 teaspoon vanilla essence

Chocolate cake

30 g ground almonds

90 g plain flour

120 g caster sugar

2 egg yolks

2 tablespoons milk

100 g dark chocolate

50 g butter

50 g walnuts

200 ml cream

Venn diagrams

1. Copy this Venn diagram. You will need to draw it much bigger than it is here.

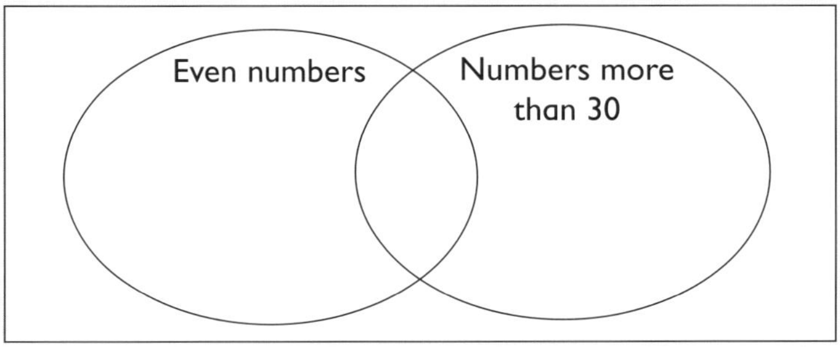

Put these numbers in the correct area in the diagram.

96	**15**	**8**	**16**	**22**	**40**	**52**	**9**
11	**73**	**5**	**18**	**27**	**130**	**29**	**57**
67	**60**	**28**	**41**	**20**	**97**	**110**	

2. Copy this Carroll diagram. You will need to draw it much bigger than it is here.

	mutiple of 3	not a multiple of 3
more than 30		
not more than 30		

Put the numbers above in the correct boxes in the Carroll diagram.

3. Make up your own Venn and Carroll diagrams and put some numbers in the correct places.

Ordering numbers

Order these numbers, smallest first.

1. 489 101 151 626 1000 818 713 982 555
1010 242 881 110 375 109 631

2. 501 191 1019 635 427 706 728 263
653 900 396 354 892 512 222 542

Order these numbers, largest first.

3. 401 181 421 626 99 1001 398 726 141
967 843 142 818 1010 1000 672 500

4. 2063 290 493 153 1013 961 873 6020
217 460 616 264 784 939 1039 507

5. Copy and complete these sequences.

61 65 69 ___ 77 ___ ___ ___

15 ___ 25 ___ 35 ___ ___

71 76 81 ___ 91 ___ ___ ___

278 276 274 ___ ___ ___ ___

384 389 394 ___ ___ ___ ___

What did you do?

Make up some sequences of your own with missing numbers

Number keys (1)

Write down the key number which is nearest to the number on each door.

Example

1. 90 → 85

1.

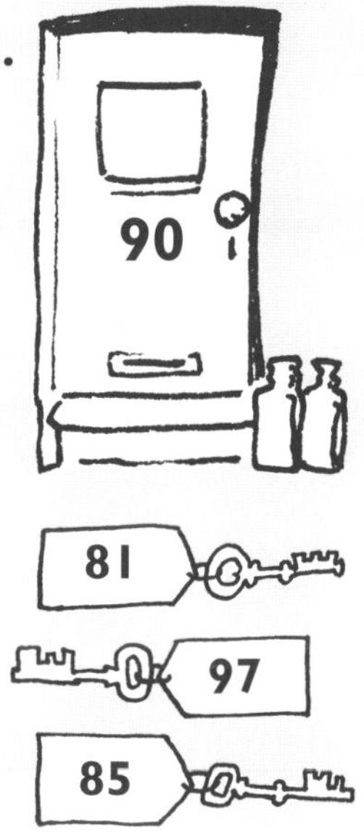

2.

3.

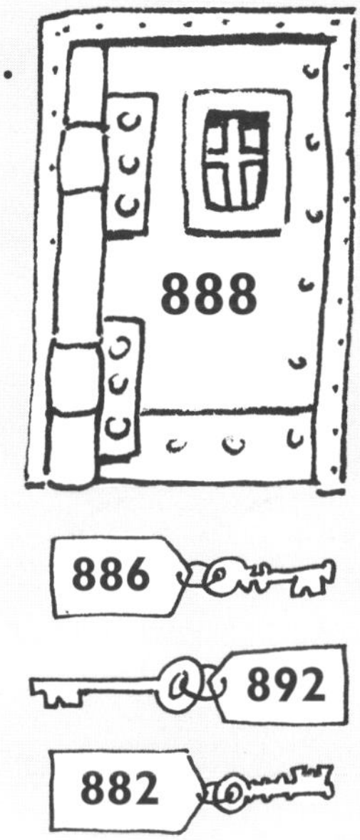

4.

5.

6.

7.

8.

Now round each door and key number to the nearest ten.

Number keys (2)

Write down the key number which is the nearest ten to the number on each treasure chest.

Example

1. 703 → 700

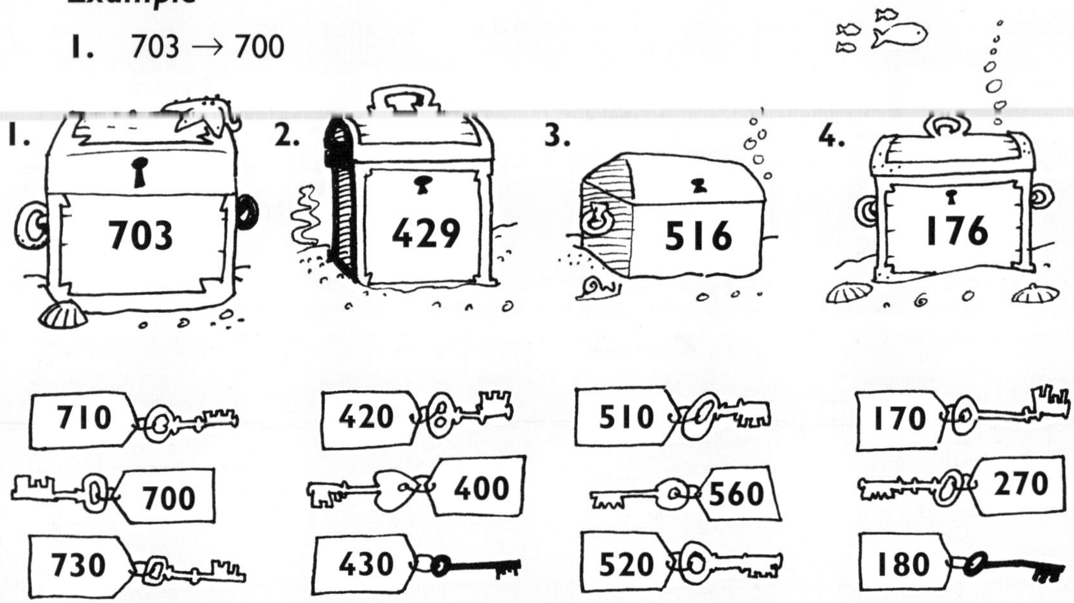

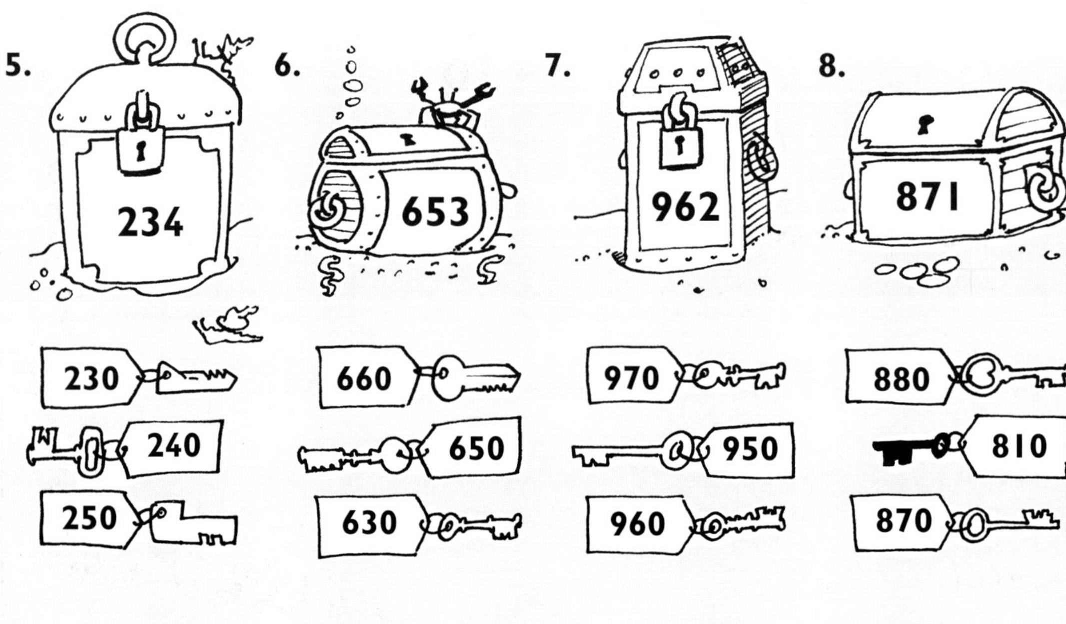

Snail paths

The snails need to reach the top of the wall. They are allowed to move in any direction horizontally, vertically or diagonally but they cannot jump over or miss a brick. They must not move backwards. Choose a snail and a route and record your score as a calculation. Each snail starts with no points. What is the highest scoring route you can find? What is the lowest scoring route?

Finish A **Finish B**

+15	+43	+29	+67	+79	
+39	−19	−8	−13	−27	−11
−0	+25	−9	+11	+17	
+15	−2	+9	−16	−8	−18
−4	−9	+12	−1	+4	
+10	−3	+10	+10	+10	+10
+13	+9	+5	+7	+12	
+8	+6	−7	−5	+5	+7
+12	+4	+16	+2	+13	

Start A **Start B**

Ray's Fish and Chips (1)

Use coins to help you.

Ten people go to Ray's Fish and Chips with different amounts of money.

Work out for each of them what they can buy, how much it will cost and how much money they will have left.

1. Anna has £3·00
2. Dominic has £2·50
3. Hardeep has £5·00
4. Naoko has £1·75
5. Jake has £2·00
6. Chloe has £4·25
7. Matthew has £4·75
8. Nazila has £10·00
9. Olly has £1·60
10. Cassie has £2·60

Ray's Fish and Chips (2)

Use coins to help you.

Ray has had a lot of complaints about mistakes in his bills.

Can you check them for him? Check the prices and the total and write out the correct bill.

1.

1 sausage	70p
1 large chips	£1·00
1 peas	55p
2 small ice creams	£1·50
Total	£4.80

2.

2 large fish	£2·25
2 large chips	£2·10
2 fizzy drinks	£2·00
Total	£6·35

3.

2 fish fingers	£1·50
2 small chips	£1·20
2 fizzy drinks	£2·00
Total	£5·70

4.

2 large fish	£1·20
1 fish fingers	75p
2 large chips	£2·00
1 large ice cream	80p
Total	£5·95

5.

1 burger	75p
1 small chips	60p
1 peas	55p
1 fizzy drink	£1·00
Total	£2·80

6.

2 large chips	£2·00
2 large ice creams	£2·00
2 orange juices	£1·50
Total	£5.00

Problems

1. Shabita has pieces of wool 35 centimetres, 52 centimetres, 1 metre, 79 centimetres and 20 centimetres long. What is the total length of all the pieces?

2. Chris is putting up posters in the classroom. He has six posters which are each 80cm wide. How wide a space does he need to put them all up next to each other?

If the classroom wall is 6 metres wide, how much space will be left?

3. Nell has started collecting a series of detective books. Each one weighs 50 grams. She has four so far. How much does her collection weigh?

Nell's older brother gives her some more books. Nell's collection now weighs 500 grams. How many books did her brother give her?

4. Tiffany is in swimming team. Every evening, she swims 500 metres. How far does she swim in a week? Write the answer in kilometres and metres.

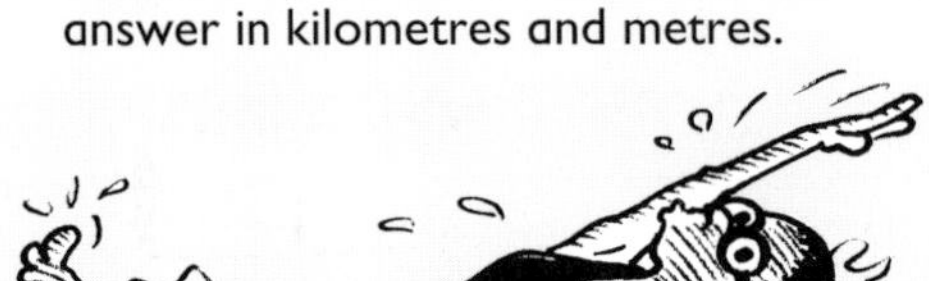

5. Susie buys pick and mix sweets for a party. She chooses 125 grams of toffees, 50 grams of cola bottles, 75 grams of jellybeans and two bars of chocolate weighing 50 grams each. What is the total weight of her sweets?

Before the party starts Susie eats half the sweets! What weight is left?

6. The doctor has given Manjeet a bottle of medicine that holds half a litre. His spoon holds 5 millilitres. How many spoonfuls of liquid are there in the bottle?

If he has to take two spoonfuls of medicine a day, how long will the bottle last?

7. Ravi's baby sister is fifteen months old. How many months until her next birthday?

How old will she be?

8. Marcus makes eighteen litres of orange squash for sports day and puts it into jugs which each hold half a litre. How many jugs will he need?

Cube building

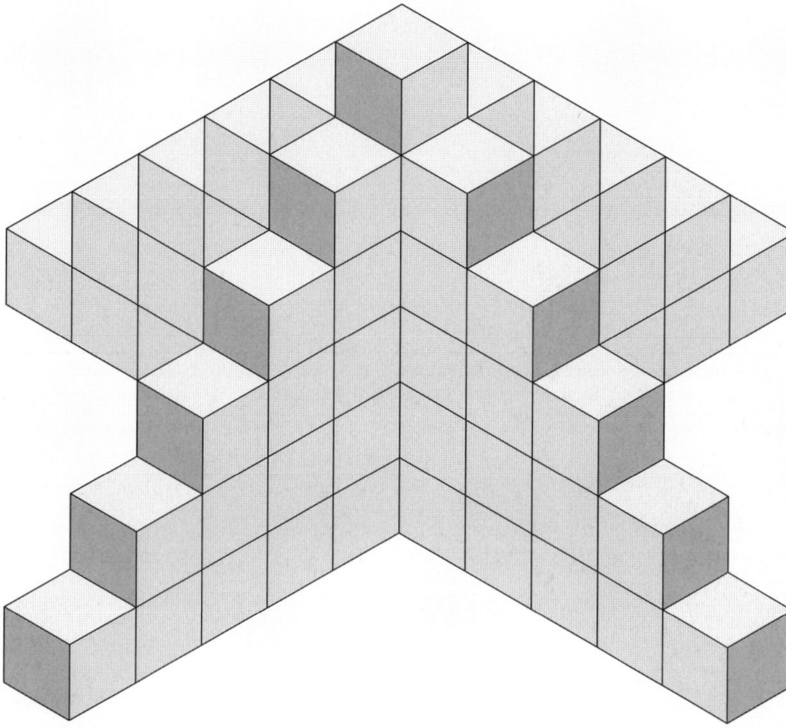

Here is a model of a building with 6 floors.

How many cubes do you need to build this model?

If you extended it to 7 floors, how many cubes would you need?

What if there were 10 floors?

Investigate.

Is there a pattern?

Ask a friend to build a model and tell them how many floors to make.

Snake Island (1)

What would you see if you stood at:

1. Viper Point and looked west?

2. the castle and looked west?

3. Cobra point and looked north?

4. the cave and looked south?

In which direction would you go to get from:

5. base camp to the woods?

6. the haunted house to the wreck?

7. the volcano to the cave?

8. the castle to the treasure?

9. base camp to the volcano?

Write the grid reference for each place.

Write the letter before the number.

Example wreck B3

10. rocks

11. cave

12. landing point

13. haunted house

14. List the squares where you would find swamp.

15. List the squares where you would find woods.

Snake Island (2)

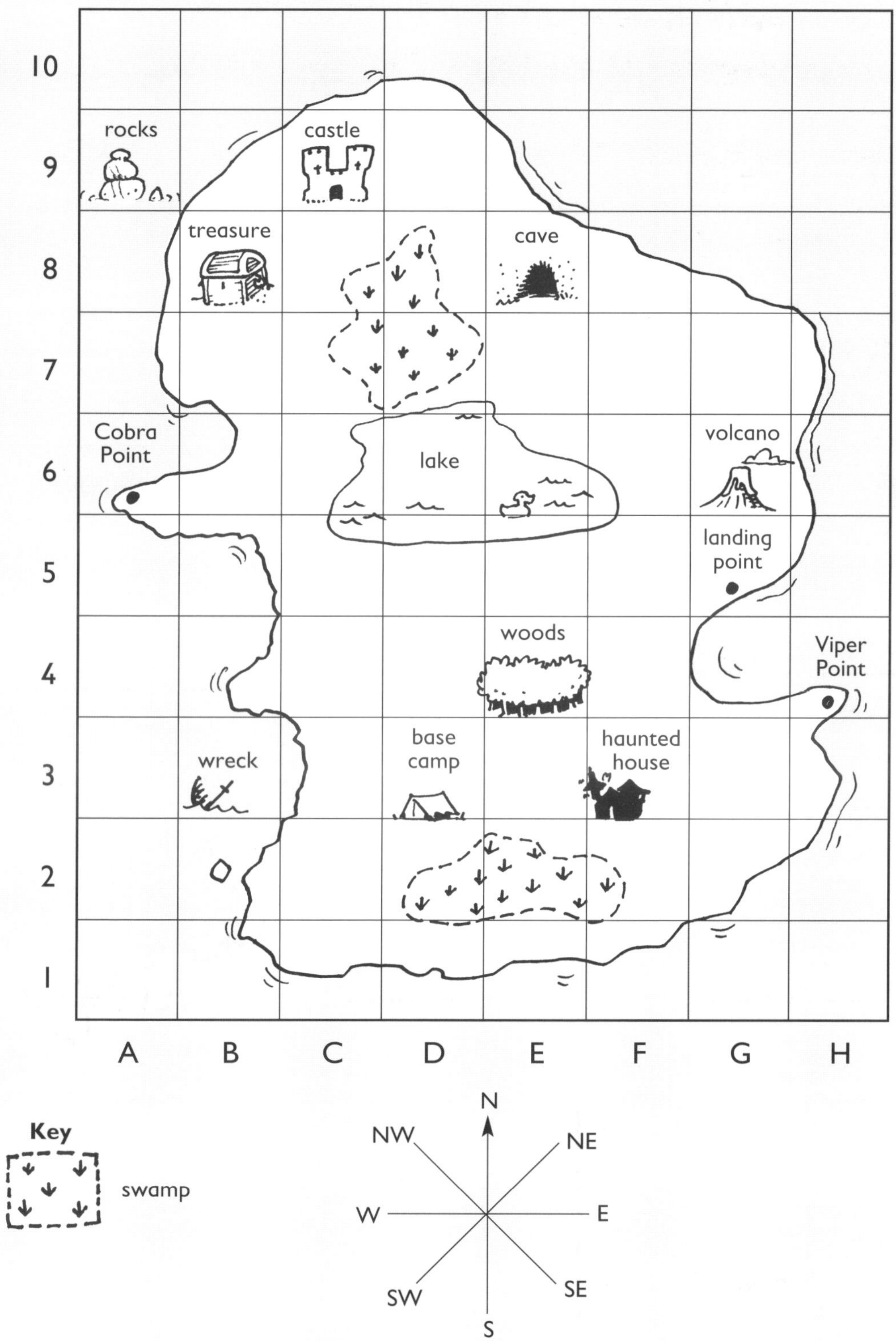

3D shapes

You may wish to work with a partner.

Here are three views of a 3D shape.

Front view

	red	
	red	
blue	blue	blue
yellow	yellow	yellow

Side view

	red
	red
blue	blue
yellow	yellow

Top view, looking down

blue	red	blue
blue	blue	blue

Can you make this shape from interlocking cubes? Look at the plans carefully.

Make your own shape and draw the plans. Give the plans to a friend to make.

Do you think that three views are enough to make a model? Do you sometimes need more views?

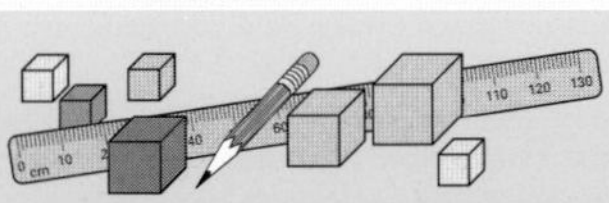

Number wheels

Write down what each letter in each number wheel stands for.

Example

1. a = 41 + 6 = 47

b = 8 + 6 = 14

c = 4 + 6 = 10 . . .

1.

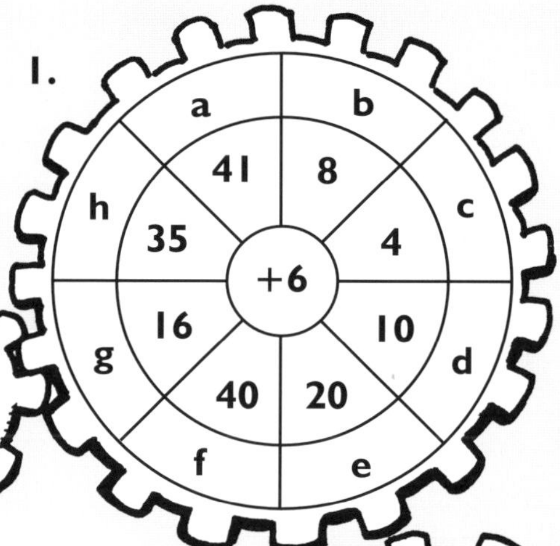

2.

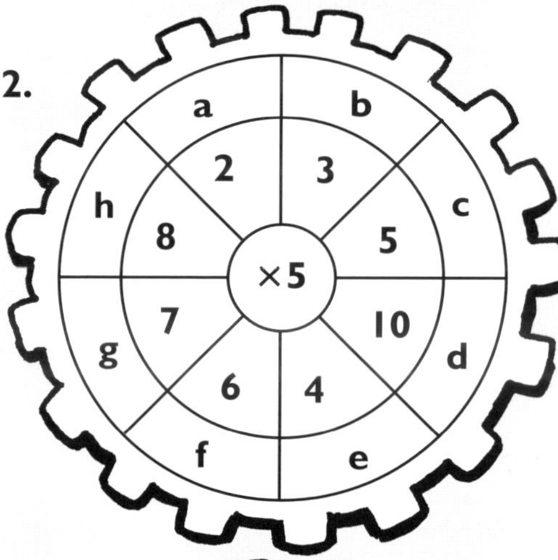

3.

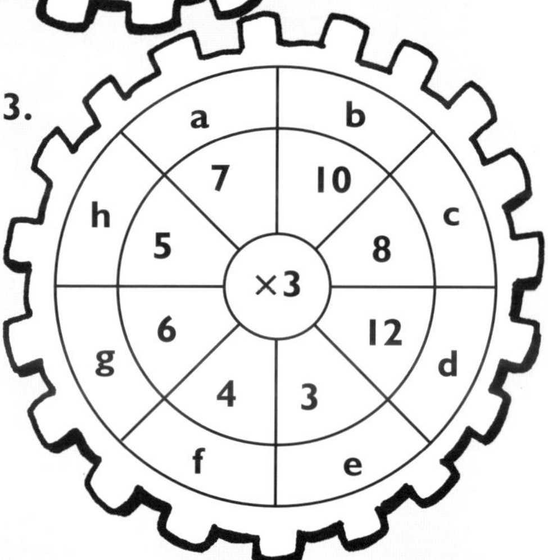

4.

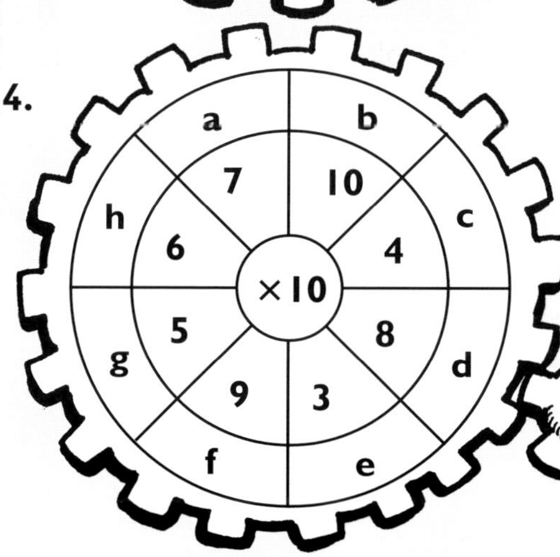

5.

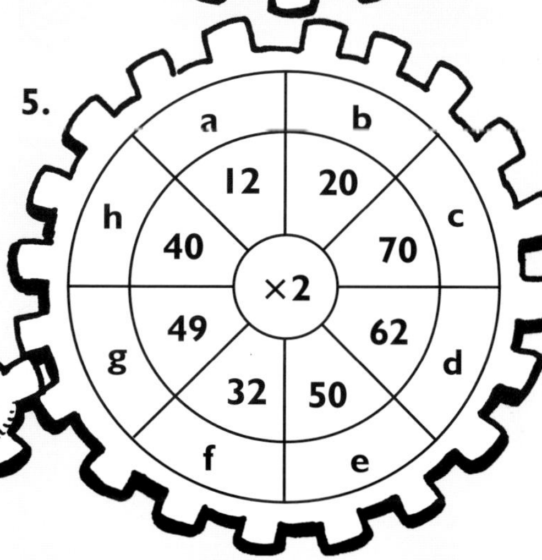

Number gates

Choose a number gate to put each set of balls through. Follow the instructions on the gate for each ball number. Write your calculations.

Example **1.** You choose the $\times 3$ gate

$12 \times 3 = 36$ $19 \times 3 = 57$ $15 \times 3 = 45$

1.

2.

3.

4.

5.

6.

7.

8.

9.

Dominoes

Place a complete set of dominoes face down on the table. Pick out four dominoes and add up how many dots there are altogether. Now try to divide your total by each of these numbers:

2 4 5 10

Each time you can divide exactly, score one point. Write down your working.

Example

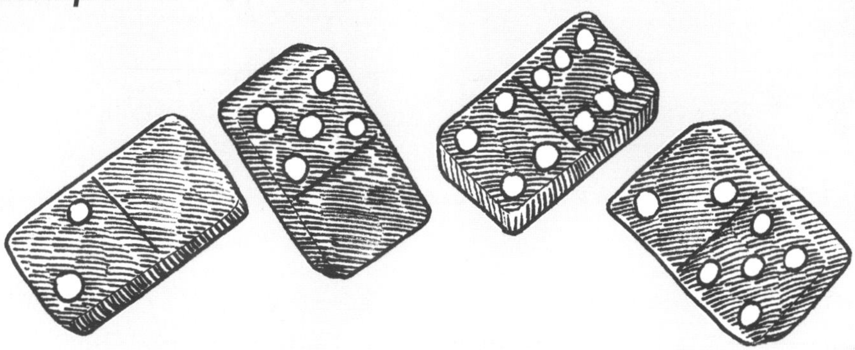

$2 + 0 + 5 + 0 + 4 + 6 + 2 + 5 = 24$

$24 \div 2 = 12$ 1 point

$24 \div 4 = 6$ 1 point

$24 \div 5 = 4$ r 4 no points

$24 \div 10 = 2$ r 4 no points

Total score = 2 points

Return the dominoes to the table, mix them up and try again with another four.

Are there any totals you can only divide by one number?

Are there any you can divide by all of the numbers?

Are there any totals which cannot be divided by any of the numbers?

School fair

How much will each stall take if they sell everything? Check your working carefully.

1.

2.

3.

4.

5.

Domino fractions

Work with a partner.

Each pair needs a set of dominoes.

Draw a grid in your workbook, like this.

Take a domino. Draw it with the smallest number at the top in the first space in your grid.

In the next space, write the domino as a fraction.

Turn the domino round the other way and draw it in the next space.

In the last space, divide the top number by the bottom number and write the answer.

If there is a remainder, don't forget to write that too.

Example

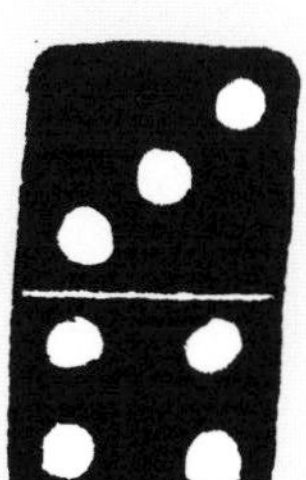	$\frac{3}{4}$	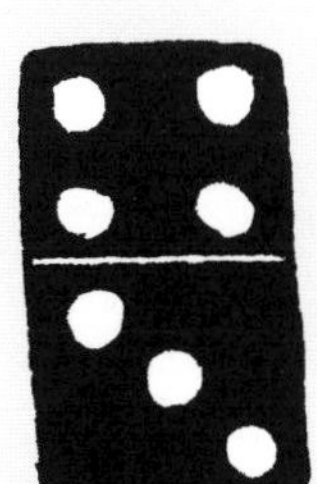	$\frac{4}{3} = 1r1$

Alien trains (1)

This is the timetable for trains on the planet Zax from Gammathorpe to Zaxville.

Station	Time	Time
Gammathorpe	9:40	10:40
Ik	10:20	11:20
Delta Junction	10:30	11:30
Kryptos	10:50	11:50
Klax	11:00	12:00
Quasartown	11:30	12:30
Zaxville	11:50	12:50

Alien trains (2)

1. If you are at Gammathorpe station at 10:00, how long would you have to wait for a train to Zaxville?

2. How long does the train take to go from Gammathorpe to Quasartown?

3. You arrive by rocket pack at Delta Junction to get the train to Klax. You arrive at 11:00. How long do you have to wait for the train?

4. How long does the train take to go from Ik to Quasartown?

5. How long does the train take to go from Kryptos to Zaxville?

6. I arrive at Ik and it is 10:10. How long do I wait for a train?

7. I just miss the 9:40 train from Gammathorpe. How long do I wait for the next one?

8. Make up two more questions using the information you have.

Mixed problems

1. I am thinking of a number. I double it and add seven. The answer is thirty-seven. What was my number?

2. Rover has 700 ml of water in his bowl. He drinks half of it, then Matt pours in another 350 ml. How much is in his bowl now?

3. Sarah has nineteen packets of instant mashed potato in a cupboard and thirty-two packets on a shelf. She uses seventeen packets. How many does she have left?

4. Sian wants to buy a computer game, which costs £8·00. She already has £2·00 and she saves 35p a week. How many weeks will she have to save?

5. I am thinking of a number. I halve it and add sixteen. The answer is forty-nine. What was my number?

6. Sunil has fifteen rose bushes in his garden. Each bush has seven flowers on it. How many flowers are there altogether?

Three more flowers appear on each bush. How many flowers altogether now?

7. Jenny sets her alarm clock for quarter to eight. When it goes off, she stays in bed for another ten minutes and then takes forty minutes to get ready for school. What time is she ready to go?

9. Simon is filling a pond that holds 50 litres of water. The jug he is using only holds 250ml. How many jugs of water will he need to fill the pond?

It takes him one minute to fetch each jug of water. How long will it take him to fill the pond?

He starts filling the pond at eleven o'clock. What time will he finish?

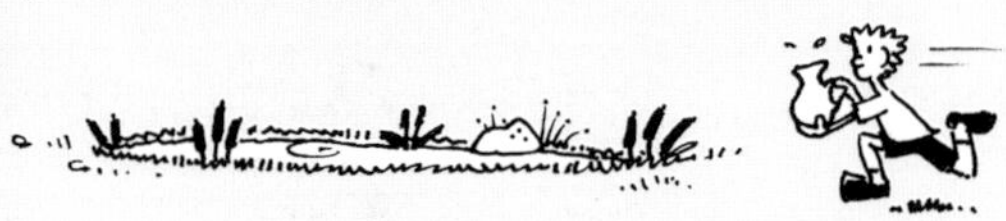